P9-DLZ-378

Me and My Pet
DOG

Christine Morley and Carole Orbell

Illustrations by
Brita Granström

WORLD BOOK / TWO-CAN

First published in the United States by
World Book Inc.
525 W. Monroe
20th Floor
Chicago IL USA 60661
in association with Two-Can Publishing Ltd.

**For information on other World Book products,
call 1-800-255-1750, x 2238.**

ISBN: 0-7166-1748-X (pbk.)
ISBN: 0-7166-1747-1 (hbk.)
LC: 96-60458

Printed in Hong Kong

1 2 3 4 5 6 7 8 9 10 99 98 97 96

Art Director: Carole Orbell
Senior Managing Editor: Christine Morley
Text: Nicole Carmichael
Additional design: Amanda McCourt and Helen Holmes
Consultant: Lisa Cobb, NCDL Animal Nurse of the Year 1995
Illustrator: Brita Granström
Photographer: Ray Moller and Rocco Rodondo
Thanks to: Tim Kelly.

Contents

Your best friend

Owning a dog can be fantastic fun. You can take it on long walks, feed and groom it, and in return it'll love you to bits! But to be a perfect dog owner, you need to know a few things about dogs...

Wild wolves

Your dog has a fearsome relative—the wolf. Thousands of years ago, some wolves gave up their wild ways and settled with humans. All the different types, or breeds, of dog you see today are relatives of these tame wolves.

Wolves are the distant ancestors of all dogs.

Most dogs are friendly and love to be cuddled.

Dogs today

In some ways, dogs still behave like wolves. They love to track a scent and chase after things that move. Wolves live together in groups that are led by one strong wolf. As your dog's owner, you are now the leader of its pack!

Perfect pals

If you look after your dog properly, it will become your best friend. Your pet will want to defend its new home against other dogs and strangers, and it will also think that you and your family are just strange-looking dogs!

Give your dog lots of love and attention, and it'll be your friend forever!

Why doesn't she have long ears like me?

Dogs, such as this basset, can smell and hear things that people can't.

All shapes and sizes

Dogs can be as small as a football or as big as you. Some breeds have long, silky hair, and others have short, curly coats. With so many different types, it can be difficult to choose your favorite!

A hundred and one dogs
Over thousands of years, dogs have been bred to help to do special tasks such as hunting, herding animals, or guarding. Some types, called lap dogs, have even been bred to be tiny, lovable companions!

I'm too big to be a lap dog.

Me too!

Some small dogs were bred to sit on their owners' laps to keep their owner warm.

I'm not afraid of you!

Feeling sheepish

Many farmers use sheep dogs to look after their flocks of sheep in the fields. A sheepdog is very obedient. It listens to its master's voice to tell it where to go and what to do.

A sheep dog has to be very fast and quick to keep the flock together.

Grrrrrrr—go away!

A lot of people use dogs to guard their home. Although you can get breeds that are very fierce and bark loudly, even a tiny dog will often try to scare off a stranger!

Get back to the flock!

Hurrah!! I've found you!

Snow rescue

St. Bernards are big, strong dogs with furry coats. They are trained to track down travelers lost in snowy mountains. Their thick coats keep them snug—even when it's freezing cold.

The right dog for you

Some dogs can live for more than 15 years, so the one you choose must be right for you. Think about how much food, exercise, and training it will need and whether you want a puppy or an adult dog.

Boy or girl?

If you buy a female dog, you should find out whether or not she has been spayed. This means she cannot have puppies. Male dogs can also have an operation to stop them from breeding.

Puppy love

Puppies are very lovable, but until they are trained they can be naughty and messy. Puppies should have their first set of shots when they are between five and eight weeks old.

Puppies are cute, but an adult dog can be just as much fun.

Choose me!

To the rescue!

One of the best places to buy a dog is from an animal shelter. Here you will find all types of dogs, and the staff can tell you about each one. If you want a particular breed, then you may have to visit someone who breeds it specially.

Home sweet home

It's important that your dog fit in with your home and family. Some dogs need lots of space to run around in, and others are content in a small apartment. If you have other pets, make sure your dog is happy to make friends!

Puppies will play happily with other animals—once they are used to them!

A healthy hound

Choose a dog that is friendly and curious. Check to see that its eyes are clear and its coat is shiny. Look into its ears to make sure they are clean.

Don't choose a dog that is much stronger than you are. Otherwise it will end up taking you for a walk!

Hurry up!

Are you ready?

At first, your dog will find its new home a bit strange, and it will want to explore every corner. Make sure you are prepared and soon it will make itself at home.

1 food bowl
2 water bowl
3 leash
4 dog tags
5 collar

Creature comfort

For the first day, keep your dog in one room. It will sniff around and explore. Make sure it has a comfy bed, fresh water, food, and a chewy toy to play with. Leave some paper on the floor or a litter box for it to use as a toilet. Spend as much time as you can getting to know your new pet.

Giving your dog a special treat will help it settle in.

I'm going to like it here!

Oooops! I've made a splash!

Danger zone!

Dogs, especially puppies, can get up to all sorts of mischief. Some will chew anything, so keep dangerous things, such as cleaning supplies, soap and electrical wires, out of their reach. Put away any valuable ornaments until your puppy is much better behaved.

Always keep your dog away from dangerous roads.

Safe and sound

Before letting your dog into the yard, make sure the gate is locked. Check to see that there are no gaps in the fence or hedge that it can wriggle through. Attach a tag with its name and your phone number to its collar, in case it gets lost.

I wonder what's out there?

Bedtime

Just as you need a warm place to sleep, your dog needs its own cosy bed. You can make one from a large, strong cardboard box and a blanket. Or you could buy a beanbag pillow or a wicker basket. Keep its bed in a quiet corner out of cold drafts and away from its food and water.

Feeling hungry

Just like people, dogs love their food! They need meat and cereals to keep them strong and healthy and to make their coats really shine.

A real dog's dinner!

Although dogs like meat, they need other kinds of food to stay healthy. An easy way to make sure your dog is eating properly is to buy dry or canned dog food from a pet or grocery store.

Canned or dry dog food that has cereal and vitamins in it makes a healthy dinner.

This beats oatmeal for breakfast!

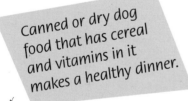

Your dog can't tell the time, but it'll know when its time for dinner!

Tasty treats

To keep their teeth healthy, dogs need something to chew on. You can buy dog chews and bones from pet stores that will do the trick. Never give your dog real bones, because they can splinter.

Don't give your dog too many treats—it will soon get fat.

The diet starts tomorrow!

Feeding time

Most grown-up dogs like to be fed once or twice a day. Puppies need to eat more often. Remember to keep separate bowls for food and water, and clean them regularly. Make sure your dog always has plenty of fresh, clean water to drink.

No scraps, please!

The dog food that you buy at the store has a mix of everything your pet needs to stay healthy—protein, cereal, and vitamins. Giving human food to your dog may make it not want its own dinner—and might make it sick, too!

Neat and tidy

Dogs are pretty good at keeping themselves clean, but every now and then they may need some help from you!

Brush and comb
Your dog will need his own set of grooming tools. Don't try using your own brush or comb!

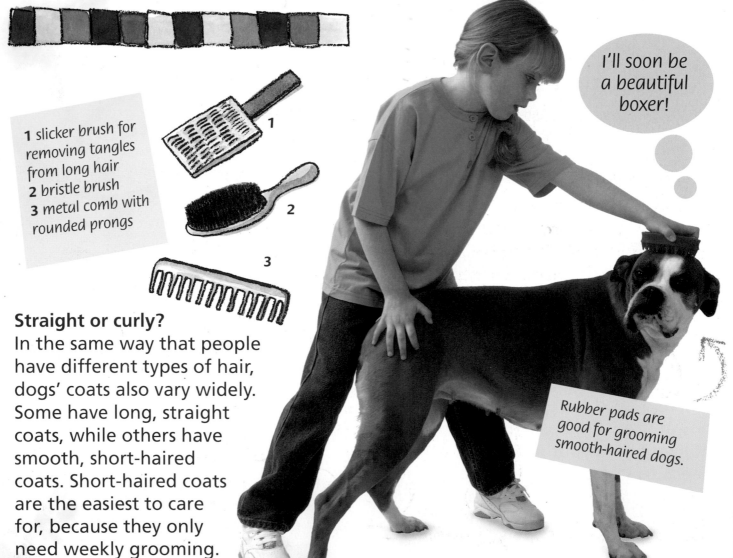

1 slicker brush for removing tangles from long hair
2 bristle brush
3 metal comb with rounded prongs

I'll soon be a beautiful boxer!

Rubber pads are good for grooming smooth-haired dogs.

Straight or curly?
In the same way that people have different types of hair, dogs' coats also vary widely. Some have long, straight coats, while others have smooth, short-haired coats. Short-haired coats are the easiest to care for, because they only need weekly grooming.

Be careful to keep soapy water out of your dog's eyes.

Bathtime

If you groom your dog regularly, it shouldn't need a bath. But if it rolls in something disgusting, a good scrub is the only solution! Use special dog shampoo and rinse it off well. Dry your pet with a towel and finish off with a blow dryer set on a low heat.

Don't use a blow dryer if your dog has itchy skin.

Not too hot—that's just right!

Head first!

As part of the grooming routine, you should gently wash your dog's ears and nose, and bathe around its eyes with a large cotton ball. Then gently brush its teeth with a special toothpaste for dogs.

Do I need any fillings?

Keeping clean

Most dogs get very excited after they've had a bath and rush around the house at top speed. It's a good idea to keep your dog indoors for a while—otherwise, it might roll in the mud all over again!

Keeping fit

Dogs need exercise just as you do. Without it, they become bored, restless and they may put on weight. Playing games is a good way to exercise your dog—and it's good fun, too!

Play away

The amount of exercise your dog needs will depend on its breed, size, and age. Dogs that spend a lot of time indoors should be allowed to run free in a safe place, away from traffic, at least once a day.

Some small dogs need just as much exercise as big ones!

OK, let's play ball!

One more tug should do it!

Walkies!

Dogs love long walks. You will have to keep your dog on a leash, and be sure to pick up after your pet with a bag or pooper scooper.

Test of strength

Playing tug-of-war with a tug toy or an old rag will give both you and your dog plenty of exercise. Don't always let your dog win a game, or it will think it's the boss!

Fetch it!

Dogs love chasing after thrown objects. Toss a ball or frisbee as far as you can and let your dog bring it back to you. Don't be surprised if your dog wants to keep this game going for a while! Only play this game in places where it is safe for your dog to be let off the leash.

Teach your dog to chase and catch a ball, and then bring it back.

Training your puppy

Puppies are clever and eager to please. This can make them easy to train! Remember to keep your lessons short, or your puppy will soon become bored!

Good dog!
You will need lots of patience when training your puppy. Whenever it does something right, make a huge fuss over it and tell it that it's a good dog. If it misbehaves, just say "No" to it in a firm voice. Never, ever hit your pet.

Who am I?
Teach your puppy its name by calling it every time you feed it. Do this when you are playing with it too. Soon it'll learn to come whenever you call its name. Remember to pat and stroke your pet when it obeys.

Call your puppy in a loud, clear voice and it'll come quickly.

Here I am!

Follow my lead

Practice walking your puppy on a leash in your backyard. Put its leash on and then walk forward slowly, calling its name. Never pull your dog. It will take some time before it can do this, so be patient.

Don't walk a young puppy too far, or it'll get very tired.

Toilet training

Your puppy will want to go to the bathroom when it wakes up in the morning and after meals. Watch out for signals such as sniffing the ground or racing around. Gently pick up your pet and place it on newspaper or take the puppy outside.

Sitting comfortably

Teach your pup to sit at mealtimes. Stand close in front of it, holding its bowl of food up high. It will have to sit down to keep looking at the bowl. If it doesn't, press its bottom down gently. Say "Sit" a few times, then praise it and give it the food.

But I haven't read the newspaper yet!

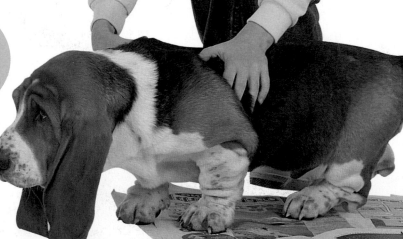

Behaving indoors

Your dog won't be very popular if it chews your shoes or chases the cat all over the house! Teach your puppy some rules to help it get along with everyone at home.

Furry friends
Dogs can get along with other pets, such as cats or guinea pigs, but it may take a while for them to get used to one another. Never leave your pets alone together until you are absolutely sure that they won't hurt each other.

I wonder if kittens like to fetch bones too?

No entry!
There are some places where your dog will not be very welcome—such as the best armchair. If you find it about to jump on a chair, say "No" firmly and lead it to its own bed. It'll soon get the message!

Puppies and kittens that grow up together can be good friends.

Naughty dog!

Sometimes your dog will pick up bad habits, such as stealing food from the table. To correct your pet, say "No" firmly and squirt a little water at it with a plant mister. Don't bother to correct your dog for something that happened a while ago— it won't remember what it did wrong!

Eeurrghh!

Use a plant mister or water pistol to correct your dog—just a little squirt will do.

Home alone

Dogs don't like being on their own for long. If they are lonely, they often bark, howl, or even chew the furniture. When you have to leave your dog alone, rub its favorite toy with your hands so that it smells like you, and then leave them together. Put the radio on too, so your pet can hear some human voices!

Don't make a fuss over your dog just before you leave—it will make your pet feel a lot worse!

Behaving outdoors

Your dog should be on its best behavior when you take it out. Teach your pet not to bark or growl at other dogs or people and to sit quietly when you leave it alone for a while.

Waiting time

Properly trained dogs will sit quietly while their owners walk away. You can practice doing this in your own yard, but never leave your dog tied up for more than a few minutes.

I'm shy

Your dog might feel a bit shy when meeting other dogs or people. To make your pet feel more brave, keep it close to you and stroke and praise it. It may take a while before it feels more confident, so be patient.

Sometimes dogs chew things when they are bored or upset at being left alone.

In the park, keep your dog on a leash until it is properly trained. In some parks, all dogs must be on a leash.

Here pup!

Good dogs always come to their owners when they are called. To teach your dog to do this, crouch down, open your arms wide and call its name. When your pet comes, give it a big hug and lots of pats. It will soon learn that coming to you is nice!

A neck scratch is the best!

Remember to make a fuss over your dog whenever it comes when you call.

Dogspeak

Dogs can "talk" to you in lots of ways—by wagging their tails, barking, panting, or even growling. Be a keen dog watcher and you'll soon learn what they're saying.

Feeling good!
Happy dogs wag their tails and point their ears forward. To make your dog really happy, scratch its back or tummy. It'll be in doggy heaven!

Most dogs love to have their tummies stroked.

Can we go out now?

Attention seeker
Dogs don't like to be ignored. When they want your attention, they may bark, howl, or tap you with their paws. They'll even try to sit close to you, putting their faces near yours!

Eeek—a bunny rabbit!

If your dog sees something it's scared of, it will flatten its ears and tuck its tail down between its legs. It might also growl and bare its teeth. If it is frightened of another animal, it will try not to look it in the eye. To stay safe, your pet might try to hide, perhaps under a table or even behind your legs!

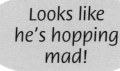

Looks like he's hopping mad!

"I'm so excited!"

When your dog is happy, it often jumps with joy. Its ears will prick up and its tail will wag furiously. It will jump up at you or run around quickly in circles. Maybe your pet thinks you're taking it for a walk in the park!

"I want to be alone"

Like people, dogs can sometimes get annoyed. You can tell that a dog is cross if it shows its teeth or growls. If a dog does this, leave it alone.

Don't disturb an old dog suddenly, especially when it is asleep. It may get cross.

Checkups

Most of the time your dog will be the picture of health. But occasionally your pet will need some help from you to keep in tip-top canine condition.

Feeling poorly

If your dog isn't eating, doesn't want to play, or is generally miserable, then it could be sick. Ask an adult to take it to the vet for a checkup. The vet will look in your dog's ears, eyes, and mouth and under its tail. The vet will also take the dog's temperature and feel its body for any lumps or bumps.

I'm a sick spaniel!

Rest and relaxation

A sick dog needs a warm, quiet place to rest. Take care of your pet by filling a hot-water bottle with warm water and tucking it under a blanket in its bed.

I feel silly!

Cool collars

When the vet gives your dog stitches or puts a bandage on its paw, she might put a large paper or plastic collar on it, too. This is called an Elizabethan collar. It will stop your dog from scratching its stitches or bandage, so that the wound will heal.

Shake flea powder onto your dog's fur, then brush it out again.

No fleas, please!

Even the cleanest dog can catch fleas, tiny black insects that live in a dog's fur. But don't worry—you can get rid of them easily with a spray, powder, or other kind of treatment offered by a vet. You can even buy special collars that help keep fleas away.

Bits and pieces

You can buy lots of useful and fun things for your dog. Some of these are helpful when you take your dog on vacation, when your pet seems bored, or when the weather turns bad.

Boredom busters

If you give your dog lots of toys, your pet will be less likely to get bored. Give it a cuddly toy or a frisbee. You can also buy treats made of rawhide. Your dog will spend hours chewing them to bits.

Never buy very small toys, because your dog might swallow them.

Puppies like soft toys that they can pick up and carry.

On the move

If you're going on an airplane trip, you can take your dog in a special travel crate. This will keep it safe and secure. Remember to put in a blanket and a toy that it can play with.

All dressed up

A dog's fur will keep it warm all year round. But if its hair is clipped or if it's really cold, you can buy your pet a coat. It will look very smart, but make sure it doesn't roll in the mud!

I wonder where I'm going?

Travel kit

Pack a bag of things your dog might need on a car trip. You should include two dishes, food, a blanket, a spare leash, and a few toys.

Amazing dogs

Dogs can do some amazing things—from starring in films to exploring the universe!

Fast forward

Some breeds of dog are very fast. The silky haired Saluki can run up to 43 miles per hour—that's faster than a car can travel in a town. A greyhound could beat a car, too.

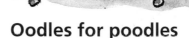

I love the wind in my ears!

Oodles for poodles

In 1931, a poodle called Toby became the world's first multimillionaire dog. He was left millions of dollars by his owner Ella Wendel of New York.

Tall tales...

The biggest dog on record was a Great Dane called Shamgret Danzas, who was $41\frac{1}{2}$ inches high!

... and tiny terriers

The smallest dog in the world was a Yorkshire terrier, just $2\frac{1}{2}$ inches high—that's about the size of a matchbox!

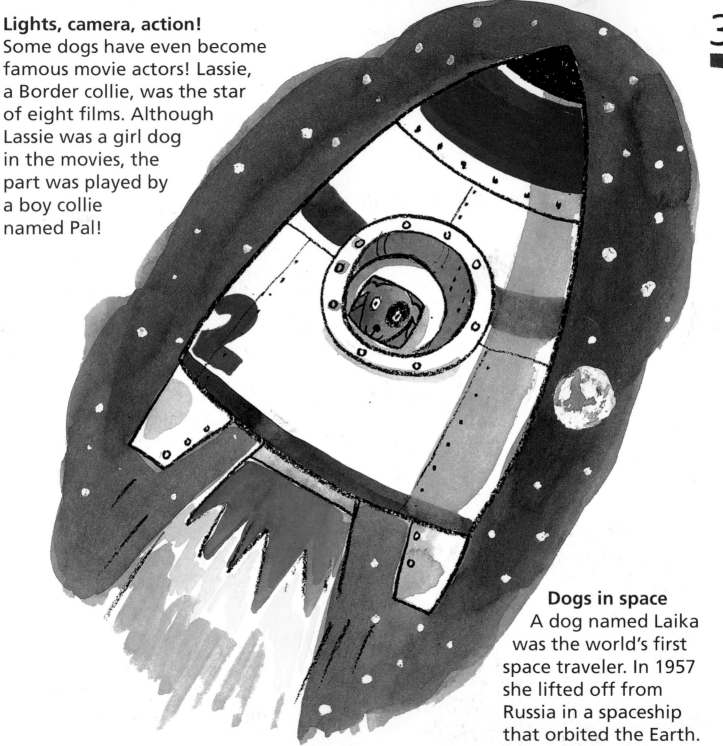

Lights, camera, action!
Some dogs have even become famous movie actors! Lassie, a Border collie, was the star of eight films. Although Lassie was a girl dog in the movies, the part was played by a boy collie named Pal!

Dogs in space
A dog named Laika was the world's first space traveler. In 1957 she lifted off from Russia in a spaceship that orbited the Earth.

Useful words

booster A **vaccination** that a dog should have once a year.

breed A type of **purebred** dog, such as a Labrador or a cocker spaniel.

canine Another word for a dog or something that is like a dog.

clip If a dog is clipped, it means its coat has been trimmed very short. Dogs with curly coats, such as poodles, are often clipped.

mongrel A dog whose parents are different breeds. Mongrels are less likely to suffer from diseases than are pedigreed dogs.

neutering An operation that dogs have to keep them from breeding. With female dogs it is called spaying. With male dogs it is called castration.

pack A group of dogs. Every pack has a leader that the other dogs obey. When dogs live with people, their owner becomes the pack leader.

pedigree A certificate that belongs to some dogs whose parents, grand-parents, and great-grandparents are all the same breed. Pedigreed dogs can be valuable and are often entered in dog shows.

puppy A dog that is less than one year old.

purebred A dog whose parents are the same breed.

vaccination This is a shot that dogs are given to stop them from getting a disease. Puppies need to get vaccinations.